The Geography of Texas

José Luis Quezada

Translated by Christina Green

Rosen
YA™
New York

Published in 2018 by The Rosen Publishing Group
29 East 21st Street, New York NY 10010

LIBRARY OF CONGRESS CATALOGING-IN-PUBLICATION DATA

Names: Quezada, José Luis.
Title: Geography of Texas / José Luis Quezada.
Description: New York : Rosen Publishing, 2018. |
Series: Explore Texas | Includes index.
Identifiers: ISBN 9781508186687 (pbk.) |
ISBN 9781508186601 (library bound)
Subjects: LCSH: Texas–Geography–Juvenile literature. |
Texas–Juvenile literature.
Classification: LCC F386.8 Q49 2018 | DDC 917.64–dc23

Manufactured in the United States of America

Contents

The Richness and Contrasts of Texas

The geography of Texas is one of the richest in the United States. Texas is the second most **expansive** state in geography, after Alaska. It also has the second largest population. This makes Texas a place with one of the greatest **contrasts** in the country and the world. Because of its urbanization, it is considered one of the most important international capitals in the world. Texas is also rich in natural resources and agricultural activity due to its extensive rural areas. Reflecting this phenomenon is the fact that Dallas and Houston are the biggest cities in the state, while Austin is the capital.

The Texas bluebonnet is the state flower.

Vocabulary

communities groups of persons or things with similar characteristics.

contrasts differences between things or persons.

expansive very large in area.

regions territories of land determined by their particular characteristics.

Texas offers many attractions for both locals and international tourists.

The richness in these geographical contrasts makes it hard to make regional classifications for Texas. Within its broad territory there are ten climatic land **regions** and eleven ecological regions. This means that in just one state there are different types of soils, topographies, geologies, precipitations, as well as vegetable, human, and animal **communities**.

Despite this diversity, Texans can all agree that the state flower is the Texas bluebonnet, the state bird is the mockingbird, and that the state mascot is the armadillo. In these pages, you will see some of the geographical marvels that Texas has to offer.

Texas has a contrasting landscape: big cities and large areas of rural land are side by side.

QUICK FACT

Texas takes up about 7.1% of the total territory of the United States.

Location of the Texas Borders

The state of Texas is located in the central south region of the United States. The land area of Texas is 268,597 square miles (695,662 square kilometers). Its **interior border** is adjacent to the states of Louisiana, Oklahoma, Arkansas, and New Mexico. Its **exterior** border is adjacent to the Mexican states of Tamaulipas, Nuevo Leon, Coahuila, and Chihuahua. Its water borders are the Gulf of Mexico and the Rio Grande.

Because Texas is a border state, it has a very wide variety of both human and physical geography.

The territorial separation between Texas and Mexico ranges from large urban areas to inhospitable deserts. One of the main separators is the Rio Grande. Another important border area is Cameron County. These two places are the most important border areas in Texas.

Migration by Mexicans and Americans through Texas is important in the study of human geography. Despite mutual benefits, there still does not exist any agreement between the two countries to regulate the flow of people.

A view of the Rio Grande.

Texas is one of the largest regions of the United States.

Other Facts

Since 2012, the migratory flow into Texas has been increasing.

The border bridge with Mexico is one of the most crossed southern border points.

Vocabulary

border the frontier between two countries or states.

exterior on the outside part.

interior on the inside part.

migration relocation of individuals or groups from one place to another.

The Texas Relief and Matagorda Bay

The Texas relief has many contrasts. On one hand, there are great mountainous extensions...

The **relief** is determined by the shapes of the land surface and the surrounding waters. There are abundant plains, hills, and plateaus in Texas. Nevertheless, the state is also rich in high elevations and **bay** areas. Prominent in its relief are the coastal and Trans Pecos areas, mainly due to their contrasts and geographical richness. The former is distinguished by its extraordinary seawater areas, such as Laguna Madre and Matagorda Bay. The latter is located in the Guadalupe Mountains, also called the **Sierra** de Guadalupe, one of the most important mountain ranges of Texas

Matagorda Bay and the Guadalupe Mountains are two of the most important geographical features located in Texas.

Matagorda Bay

- Located on the Texas coast.

- Home to the ghost town Indianola, a port destroyed in the nineteenth century by hurricanes.

- Its fertile soil promotes wildlife and seafood production, which attracts tourism.

...and on the other hand, it has one of the longest coastal zones in the country.

Other Facts

Matagorda Bay has interesting historical episodes based on its foundation and construction stages:

● **The first records of European navigators called it the Holy Spirit Bay.**

● **In 1685, the French explorer Rene-Robert Cavelier established the Fort St. Louis Colony on the coast of the bay.**

● **In 1722, the Spanish built a fort called the Presidio La Bahía and the Misión de Nuestra Señora del Espíritu Santo de Zúñiga.**

● **In 1831, Linnville was the main port of the Republic of Texas.**

Very Interesting!

Texas has the third longest coastline of the United States.

The Guadalupe Mountains

● It is located in western Texas.

● The highest point in Texas—Guadalupe **Peak**—is located in the Guadalupe Mountains.

● Another famous Texas peak, named El Capitan, is also located in this range.

Texas has many long coastlines, along which some big cities are located.

Climate in Texas and in Its Main Cities

The **climate** in Texas varies a lot due to its enormous territorial expansiveness. The climatic diversity varies in precipitation and temperature depending on the latitude and **altitude**. This climatic variation can be seen in its historical maximum and minimum temperatures.

On August 12, 1936, the **hottest** temperature ever in Texas was recorded at 120.2° F (49° C) in Seymour, a city in Baylor County.

On February 12, 1899, the coldest temperature was recorded at -23.8° F (-31° C) in Tulia, a city in Swisher County.

Houston, San Antonio, and Dallas are the most well known cities in Texas, and therefore it is important to know their climate types.

Houston

● Has a subtropical climate.

● In the summer the temperature can reach 94° F (34° C).

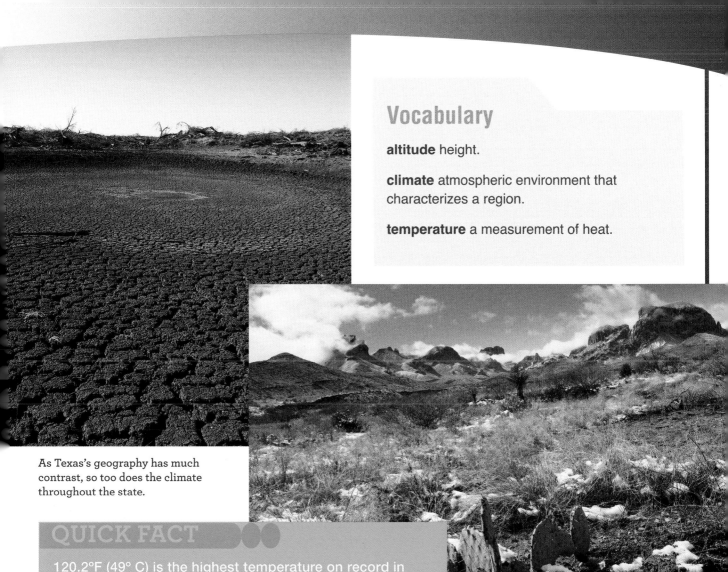

Vocabulary

altitude height.

climate atmospheric environment that characterizes a region.

temperature a measurement of heat.

As Texas's geography has much contrast, so too does the climate throughout the state.

QUICK FACT

120.2°F (49° C) is the highest temperature on record in Texas, while the lowest on record is -23.8° F (-31° C).

San Antonio

● Has a dry and humid climate.

● The summers are hot and the winters can be either mild or cold.

● The temperature in San Antonio has reached as high as 110.2° F (43.9° C).

Dallas

● Has a subtropical humid climate.

● The summers are very hot and temperatures often exceed 104° F (40° C).

Important Rivers and Bodies of Water

Pennybacker Bridge in Austin.

Texas is **irrigated** by some 3,700 rivers, 180 lakes and reservoirs, and 15 river systems totaling 191.29 mi. (307.85 km). All of the rivers in the state flow into the Gulf of Mexico. The three longest of these are the Rio Grande, the Red River, and the Brazos River. Texas is rich in other aquiferous bodies, such as **lakes**, caves, and **swamps**.

It is interesting to learn about some characteristics of two of the most important bodies of water in the state: the Rio Grande and Caddo Lake.

The Frio River gives its name to Frio County.

Río Grande

● Of its 1885 mi. (3,034 km), 1254 mi. (2018 km) run along border between the United States and Mexico.

● It passes through Colorado, New Mexico, and Texas in the United States, and the Chihuahua, Coahuila, Nuevo Leon, and Tamaulipas Mexican states.

● It is neither a navigable nor a touristic river.

QUICK FACT ●●●

The greatest concentration of lakes in the world is found on the Southern High Plains of Texas.

Vocabulary

irrigated supplied with water.

lakes bodies of water surrounded by land.

swamps marshlands.

The San Antonio River flows through the city bearing its name. There are many businesses located along its route for an enjoyable walk.

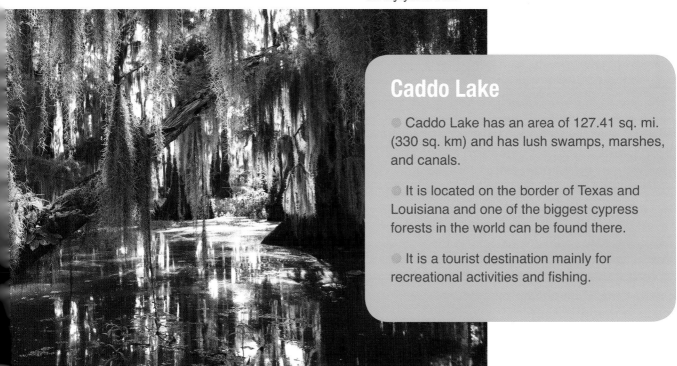

Caddo Lake

● Caddo Lake has an area of 127.41 sq. mi. (330 sq. km) and has lush swamps, marshes, and canals.

● It is located on the border of Texas and Louisiana and one of the biggest cypress forests in the world can be found there.

● It is a tourist destination mainly for recreational activities and fishing.

Natural Regions of Interest

Geological formations in Caprock Canyon.

Texas is divided into many natural regions, including coastal plains, eastern pine forests, interior lowlands, the great plains, and western Texas.

Within these regions, we can find tropical forests, arid zones, and semi-arid zones. A great part of the **biodiversity** of Texas is concentrated here. Throughout Texas we can find bays, protected lagoons, pine forests, deserts, and the famous Rocky Mountains.

Due to their history and how well they represent these five regions, Corpus Christi Bay and the Staked Plain are worthy special mention.

Very Interesting!

The Spanish conquistador Francisco Vázquez de Coronado was the first European to enter the region in 1541. He described the Staked Plain with these words:

"I have encountered plains so vast that I have not been able to discern their limits anywhere, even after travelling 300 leagues... with no further land indications, as if they had all been swallowed by the sea... there was not a single rock, nor elevated land, nor a tree, nor a bush, nor anything to walk past".

Corpus Christi Bay

- This is a semi-**tropical** bay on the coast of Texas. It is located in the counties of San Patricio and Nueces.

- It covers approximately 308 sq. mi. (497 sq. km).

- In addition to being a touristic destination due to its location, it is an area for military establishments and industry, where an abundance of oil and natural gas can be found.

Vocabulary

biodiversity variety of animal and vegetable species in an environment.

plateau an extensive plain located at an elevated height above sea level; a mesa.

tropical relating to the tropics.

Staked Plain

- This is one of the biggest plateaus in the United States and covers an approximate area of 37,500 sq. mi. (97,000 sq. km).

- Some of its most important parts are found in the northwest of Texas and parts of New Mexico.

- Its original name comes from Spanish: Llano Estacado.

- The Caprock Escarpment defines the northern limit of this **plateau**.

Many birds find shelter on the coasts of Texas, especially in the Aransas National Wildlife Refuge.

Two Emblematic Landscapes

Due to the expanse of its territory, Texas has diverse landscapes that are identified as part of the southwest of the United States. From the perspective of ecological tourism, this environmental wealth offers such varied features as beaches, deserts, and mountains.

Currently, Texas is one of the ten most visited states in the United States. It has 1.57 million **tourists** per year experiencing it geographical and climatic resources. Two places that are emblematic of the climatic contrasts of Texas are King **Ranch** and Padre Island.

King Ranch

- This is the biggest ranch in the United States and among the biggest properties in the world.

- It has an area of 825,000 acres (333,865 hectares), making it bigger than the Island of Tenerife and the state of Rhode Island.

- The Nueces River and Rio Grande flow through it, and it shares a border with Mexico.

A beach on Padre Island.

Padre Island

- Located on the southern coast of Texas.

- It is the longest **sandbar** in the world, measuring about 130 mi. (210 km) in length.

- It is located in the counties of Cameron, Kenedy, Nueces, and Willacy.

Texas offers beautiful landscapes, where ranches are sometimes located.

Vocabulary

ranch a farm for work and recreation where animals are often raised.

sandbar a sandy shoal in the sea.

tourists people who visit locations.

Fireworks on Padre Island.

Important Parks and Ecological Zones

Guadalupe Mountains National Park

- Located at the Guadalupe Mountain Range in western Texas and southeastern New Mexico.

- Founded on September 30, 1972.

- Guadalupe Peak, the highest point in Texas, is found here, with an elevation of 8,751 feet (2,667 meters).

- El Capitan is also one of the emblematic peaks of this park.

Texas has a system of national **parks** and nature **reserves** that allows visitors to appreciate the **majesty** of its geography as well as the wealth of plant and animal life. Currently there are more than 120 state parks that cover a total of 945.95 sq. mi. (2,450 sq. km.). Because of the height of their summits, the two most important parks in western Texas are the Guadalupe Mountains National Park and the Big Bend National Park. It is worth knowing more details and characteristics of these two emblematic places.

Very Interesting!

The five most important national parks in Texas are E.O. Siecke, I.D. Fairchild, John Henry Kirby Memorial, Masterson, and W. Goodrich Jones.

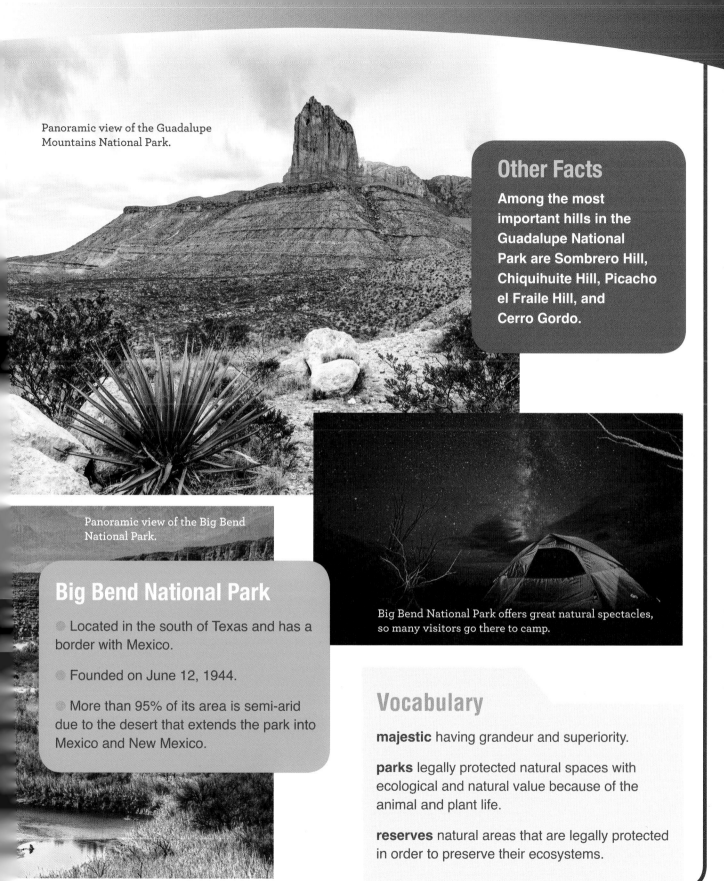

Panoramic view of the Guadalupe Mountains National Park.

Panoramic view of the Big Bend National Park.

Big Bend National Park

- Located in the south of Texas and has a border with Mexico.

- Founded on June 12, 1944.

- More than 95% of its area is semi-arid due to the desert that extends the park into Mexico and New Mexico.

Big Bend National Park offers great natural spectacles, so many visitors go there to camp.

Vocabulary

majestic having grandeur and superiority.

parks legally protected natural spaces with ecological and natural value because of the animal and plant life.

reserves natural areas that are legally protected in order to preserve their ecosystems.

Plants and Animals

The bison is a protected species in Texas.

The red wolf is in danger of extinction.

Texas has many native birds and animals along with **species** introduced by man. There are more than 550 species of birds in the state. This means that three-quarters of all the species in the United States can be found in Texas. In addition, there are many types of indigenous snakes, some of which are dangerous, like the rattlesnake and the water moccasin. The government of Texas takes measures to prevent the **extinction** of several of its most valuable species. Some of these are the bison, the American black bear, the puma, and the red wolf.

The armadillo is a representative species of Texas.

The Armadillo

This mammal is considered to be the Texas state **mascot** and is found throughout the state, except in the western Trans Pecos region.

The Red Wolf

Despite its protected species status, this mammal is on the road to extinction. The few that remain are found in captivity. Its natural habitat was the western part of Texas. The red wolf, along with the grey wolf, are on the state and federal endangered species list.

Vocabulary

extinction when something terminates or disappears forever.

mascot an animal thought to bring good luck.

species a group of persons, animals, or things that are similar to each other.

Human Geography

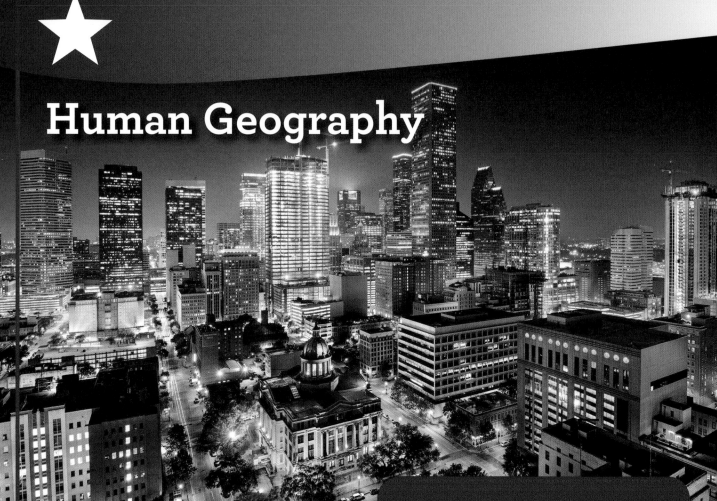

Human geography is the study of societies in spaces, the relationship among each other and physical media, as well as cultural and regional landscapes that human beings construct. Human geography in Texas is understood from the study of its cities, rural habitats, and its **urbanization**.

After the Second World War, Texas and its cities grew in population and in economy. Based on the census for the year 2000, more than 80% of Texans reside in urban areas. Currently, the most populated cities are Houston, San Antonio, and Dallas.

QUICK FACT

Houston is the fourth largest city in the United States.

Very Interesting!

The city of Houston was founded on June 5, 1837. Its origin is interesting: in 1836, the brothers John and Augustus Allen, after purchasing lands from the Mexican government, decided to name the city in honor of Samuel Houston, the leader of the Battle of San Jacinto who was also the president of Texas in September 1836.

Vocabulary

urbanization when a land is conditioned and prepared for urban use: streets are lighted and paved, and other services are offered.

Glossary

altitude height.

bay a natural inlet from the sea.

biodiversity variety of animal and vegetable species in an environment.

border the frontier between two countries or states.

climate atmospheric environment that characterizes a region.

communities groups of persons or things with similar characteristics.

contrasts differences between things or persons.

expansive very large in area.

exterior on the outside part.

extinction when something terminates or disappears forever.

interior on the inside part.

irrigated supplied with water.

lakes bodies of water surrounded by land.

majestic having grandeur and superiority.

mascot an animal thought to bring good luck.

migration relocation of individuals or groups from one place to another.

parks legally protected natural spaces with ecological and natural value because of the animal and plant life.

peak the highest part of a mountain.

plateau an extensive plain located at an elevated height above sea level; a mesa.

ranch a farm for work and recreation where animals are often raised.

regions territories of land determined by their particular characteristics.

relief a group of landforms on the surface of the Earth.

reserves natural areas that are legally protected in order to preserve their ecosystems.

sandbar a sandy shoal in the sea.

sierra a mountain chain with hills and cliffs.

species a group of persons, animals or things that are similar to each other.

swamps marshlands.

temperature a measurement of heat.

tourists people who visit locations.

tropical relating to the tropics.

urbanization when a land is conditioned and prepared for urban use: streets are lighted and paved, and other services are offered.

Index